Northampton

in old picture postcards

by
Lou Warwick
and
Alan Burman

Third edition

European Library - Zaltbommel/Netherlands MCMLXXXVIII

GB   ISBN 90 288 3419 2 / CIP

© 1986 European Library - Zaltbommel/Netherlands

European Library in Zaltbommel/Netherlands publishes among other things the following series:

IN OLD PICTURE POSTCARDS *is a series of books which sets out to show what a particular place looked like and what life was like in Victorian and Edwardian times. A book about virtually every town in the United Kingdom is to be published in this series. By the end of this year about 300 different volumes will have appeared. 1,500 books have already been published devoted to the Netherlands with the title* **In oude ansichten.** *In Germany, Austria and Switzerland 650, 100 and 25 books have been published as* **In alten Ansichten;** *in France by the name* **En cartes postales anciennes** *and in Belgium as* **In oude prentkaarten** *and/or* **En cartes postales anciennes** *150 respectively 400 volumes have been published.*

For further particulars about published or forthcoming books, apply to your bookseller or direct to the publisher.

PREFACE

In the 43rd year of the reign of Queen Victoria Northampton was a much, much smaller town than today, despite having more than doubled its population in the half-century before 1880. It still had the 'feel' of an enlarged village and in fact cattle were still grazing in fields quite near to the town centre. Many of the districts of terraced streets had yet to be built, mainly with the aid of the Freehold Land and Building Society, then 32 years old. This strictly local concern later became Northampton Town and County Benefit Building Society which in turn metamorphosed into the gigantic Anglia Building Society.

There were some 50,000 Northamptonians in 1880 and the younger ones were to be the first to benefit from the new compulsory State Education in schools then being erected such as Military Road. Until that year parents had been able to please themselves whether their offspring should receive a formal education. Now the youngsters had to attend school, most staying until they were 12.

In the streets the horse reigned supreme although there were some bicycles. During the 1880s horse trams were to supplant horse buses. The town was about to acquire its third railway station, on the site of the ancient castle, which would, as a local newspaper put it, 'make the town a suburb of London'. Many Northamptonshire villages had their own stations and more were to be put on to the railway map with the construction of the Great Central Line in the 1890s.

Before the 50 years time-span of this book were out five villages near to Northampton were to lose their independence to the civic embrace of the Borough.

The shops of the Northampton of 1880 were nearly all local and most of the owners lived on the premises. Early closing movements sought to persuade them to close at 8 p.m. and in 1881 drapers and tailors made the concession of closing on the Thursday half-day at the early hour of 4!

In 1882 the first successful demonstration of electric light took place on the Market Square but gas was to hit back with the incandescent mantle and hold the new fuel at bay for many years.

In 1880 the modest Theatre Royal in Marefair was on its last legs. The true Victorian atmosphere might be found there on a Saturday night, as the Northampton Albion had reported in 1875, with those in the gods not only dropping orange peel and other refuse on to those in the pit but also 'at one time a piece of lighted paper came floating down, much to the horror of nervous people'. In four years time townsfolk were having to pinch themselves that they were not in London as they sat in the first night audience at the much larger and more handsome Royal Theatre in Guildhall Road on Monday, 6 May 1884.

But perhaps the most surprising rural touch to the Northampton of 1880 is that at least one windmill was still turning in the area occupied by the expanded town of 1986. The one at Wootton was, in fact, still working until 1905. And one in Market Street had been operational until shortly before our startpoint year.

The compilers of this collection, Warwick and Burman, are journalist and photographer respectively but make no apology for suggesting that the most important development in the Northampton of 1880 was the starting up of daily local newspapers in a town which had already been blessed with weekly printed sheets for the remarkable period of 160 years, the Northampton Mercury having been first published in 1720.

Without photographers there would not, of course, have been the raw material to construct this book. You could in 1880 have the choice of several local studios in which to have your picture taken. Indeed, the pioneer one had been set up as early as 1844 when Mr. Whitlock opened up in Mercers Row and the Northampton Mercury praised 'a fidelity which is absolutely startling – there is no more the possibility of mistaking the likeness than there is of mistaking the reflection of an individual in a looking glass'. And taking the picture occupied only 'the space of five seconds... on a bright day'.

We do not, as far as we know, have any of Mr. Whitlock's photographs in this book but we acknowledge and salute all those of his colleagues, professional and amateur, whose creations have come our way. There is not in every case the means of knowing which cameraman was responsible, but quite a few are by Henry Cooper, who was in business in George Row for many years.

1. Although dating from two centuries before the time span of this book this scene is included because it is an unusually fine impression of a provincial town in the 17th century. It was drawn by an artist in the entourage of Prince Cosmo, a visitor in 1669. The Prince, who was to become Cosmo III, Grand Duke of Tuscany, had been sent on the trip by his father, Ferdinand II, to get him away from his turbulent wife. The Northampton call was part of a Grand Tour including Spain and Portugal. As this unique drawing shows the central church of All Saints, due for destruction six years later in the dreadful fire of Northampton in 1675, originally stretched as far west from the then central tower as to the east. Glimpsed on the right is the then South Bridge.

GEORGE HOTEL. NORTHAMPTON

2. As well as an artist Prince Cosmo brought a diarist who recorded that he stayed at the Inn of St. George – the George Hotel which was also to be destroyed in the fire six years later. This early 20th century picture of its successor, taken by Henry Cooper, shows the George, at the corner of George Row and Bridge Street, in its final days of glory for it stood derelict for several years before being pulled down and replaced by Lloyds Bank in the 1920s. In the 18th century its rooms were not numbered but had names, including the Queen's Head Chamber, King's Head, Mermaid, Crown, Globe, Mitre and Rose. In the 19th century it was the last property in England to be disposed of by the 'Tontine' system whereby the last survivor(s) of the subscribers inherited the building.

3. Victorian scene on the Market Square. Before Newland was widened Gray's Millinery Establishment occupied the narrow building on the corner, next to the arched frontage which was later the offices of the Northampton Mercury (founded 1720) and Daily Echo (1880) but which was then occupied by Hall, Shawl and Mantle, and Mobbs, Snow and Wood. Next to the Peacock Hotel on the right (east side) were Ingham's Eating House, Lester's, and the Lord Palmerston public house, which had been known as the Flying Horse until soon after Palmerston's death in 1865. He had visited the town and Lady Palmerston 'cut the first sod' of the East and West Junction railway line at Towcester in 1864. In recent times the pub gave way to Huckleberry's and Wimpy's fast food establishments. Other pubs on the Square at various times included the Three Tuns, Post Horn, British Banner, Admiral Rodney, Greyhound, Trooper and the Windmill (renamed the Queen's Arms in honour of the Accession of Queen Victoria but now replaced by a betting shop).

4. Captain Samuel Isaac, who gave the celebrated former Fountain which stood on Northampton Market Square from 1863 to 1962, is seated on the left of this group of the 5th Northamptonshire Rifle Volunteers, of which he was Captain Commandant. They are pictured on their return from Belgium in 1866, where they gained the decorations they are wearing. Next to Isaac is Captain J. Macquire, founder of the auctioneering firm of Macquire, Tarry and Merry. On the right of the rear row is Sergeant J. Hughes who later became Captain Quarter-Master. A Jew, Captain Isaac was a member of the shoe firm of Isaac, Campbell and Co. of Campbell Square, and stood unsuccessfully for Parliament. The steps of the Fountain became a forum for speakers, George Bernard Shaw and Charles Bradlaugh M.P. being among those who held forth there.

5. Carriages are drawn up on the Parade, on the north side of the Market Square. Leamington House was probably so called because the Franklins came from that town. For many years J.E. Franklin ran a bakery and confectioners in part of the premises which were also the headquarters of the Northampton Mercury. The firm moved to Guildhall Road in 1873 being then described as a wine and spirit merchant. There the Franklins Restaurant and Hotel had been erected by Edmund Franklin whose brother, John Campbell Franklin, built the nearby Royal Theatre and Opera House in 1884. Today the former hotel is used as the headquarters of the Northamptonshire Community Youth Affairs Bureau.

6. After the Franklins had left the Parade, Leamington House was renamed Parade House and was the home of the china and glass firm of W.T. Church, begun by Thomas Church in Devizes in 1849. Hostility towards his Non-conformist views had led to the move to Northampton where he operated in Bridge Street in about 1858. Next came moves to the Drapery and, in about 1865, to the Parade. About the turn of the century the firm had notice to quit to make way for the erection of the Emporium Arcade but returned to take premises at the Market Square entrance to the Arcade in 1911... only to be driven out again 60 years later when the Arcade was demolished to provide a site for the Grosvenor Centre. Today the firm is in the rebuilt Welsh House next to the entrance to the Centre.

Bird's-Eye View Market Square Northampton.

7. View of the Market Square from the tower of All Saints Church about 1905 with the Emporium Arcade then dominating the north side of the Square. The Mercury and Echo newspapers had moved into the arched building next door and on the other side the narrow building was still standing at the entrance to Newland. It was demolished in street widening of about 1910. Formerly occupying the Fountain's position had been a Market Cross of octagonal form with steps leading to a room in which the standard weights and measures were deposited. Erected in 1535 this was destroyed in the fire of 1675. From 1780 to 1805 an obelisk stood there and later an iron pump which was moved to Cheyne Walk when the Fountain was installed.

8. A wider entrance to Newland is seen in this Market Square view. On the other side of the Arcade were the premises of Abel's music shop which had been there since 1794 when Mr. J. Abel began a bookshop. In 1800, long before the days of public libraries, he provided a 'subscription general library'. By 1817 the shop was a wonderland for musicians for in addition to pianos and square pianos there was 'the largest assortment of double basses, violincellos, tenors, violins, bass drums, bassoons, serpents, tenoroons, hautbois, clarinets, flutes, flageolets, rarely to be met with in one shop' and in 1846 the firm was granted the Royal Arms and in 1863 the Prince of Wales' feathers. The firm closed in 1970.

9. Situated since 1937 in the Abington Square Garden of Rest War Memorial the Mobbs Memorial seen here was originally on the Market Square in front of the premises of the Northampton Herald and Daily Chronicle. Lt. Col. Edgar Mobbs, DSO, was killed at Ypres, France, in 1917. A Saints rugby player with seven England caps he had been turned down as 'too old' when he volunteered at 35. He then formed his own company of 260, known as the 7th Northamptonshires or Mobbs Battalion. The Herald had been founded in 1831 and the Chronicle in 1880. An inscription on the back of this picture reads: 'Where Charles Stopford first met Audrey Robinson.' Charles Stopford was on the accounting staff from 1912-1916 while Audrey Robinson was Northampton's first woman reporter and was there from 1916-1928. The pair married and became Mayor and Mayoress of Northampton in 1971. (Photo: C. Smith, St. James Road.)

10. Many a speech was made from two Market Square platforms seen in this picture by Alan Burman – the balcony of the Peacock Hotel, on the east side, and the steps of the Fountain. A document in the County Record Office at Delapre Abbey mentions the sale of 'Le Pecok' on 8 February 1456. The last drinks were consumed on 27 May 1956, and the building was demolished four years later to make way for the Peacock Way shopping arcade which in 1986 is itself in turn awaiting demolition. The balcony was saved and included in the Chapel Brampton bungalow home of Mr. E.C.M. Palmer, chairman and managing director of the last owners of the hotel, Phipps Northampton Brewery Co. Ltd., then being absorbed by Watney Mann Ltd. Several 18th and 19th century landlords of the inn became Mayors of Northampton. This picture was taken in the 1950s.

11. Horse-cabs in the Drapery. The premises on the left are those of Adnitt Brothers, now replaced by Debenhams. An interesting aspect of this picture is the way in which the Parade used to project into Sheep Street. In fact there were two stages of widening and rounding off this corner to ease the passage of vehicles. The first was in the 1670s after the dreadful fire of Northampton had burned down three quarters of the town. The second involved new premises for Hollis's which are seen in a later picture. Note the 'Horse Cattle and Dog Medicines' establishment next to Hollis's.

12. The corner of the Drapery and Mercers Row in the early 1920s. This was where the Westminster Bank building, now occupied by the Anglia Building Society, was erected in 1925. The Drapery was so called because drapers occupied the west side in the 14th century, the other side being known then as the Glovery, because glovers were working there.

13. A dray with a barrel aboard stands in Mercers Row when businesses operating included James Brothers' grocery shop and Lankester and Wells wines and spirits. At the far end stands Spoors Corner, at the lower end of Abington Street. In a letter telling his recollections of events in early Victorian times John Marlow wrote to the Northampton Mercury in 1890: 'There was only one fish shop in the town and that was on Wood Hill on the site now occupied by Messrs. Mackintosh,' which can be seen in this picture. He went on: 'It was a very old-fashioned place you having to go up three or four steps and all the fish they had came by coach, and that some-times would be only a small hamper. That had to supply the town, it was equally divided among the gentry and there was no cheap fish in those days.'

14. Wood Hill was so called because a wood market was held there. At the time this picture was taken it was the start point for several of the carrier's carts which provided passenger and goods transport to the villages. In 1890, recalling the times of several decades earlier, John Marlow said: 'On Wednesdays and Saturdays Wood Hill was busy for the woodmen from Silverstone and the carriers from the country would take up parts of the road and Worsters and Stubbs' large meat wagons would be loaded with hampers of meat for the London Market, sometimes several rows one upon the other.' A weighing machine also stood there on which coal was weighed before delivery to the County Goal, Infirmary and Workhouse. It was removed in 1890.

15. Wood Hill later became a starting point for motor taxis and for buses. By then the town's first public lavatories had been built there, underground. After the First World War there was a public subscription for a local limbless ex-serviceman named Eckford. From this a news kiosk was bought and erected in front of All Saints Church but by the time this picture was taken it had been moved to Wood Hill, behind the church. Note how Waterloo House, glimpsed behind 'Eckford's Kiosk', had replaced the old Duke of Clarence public house.

16. Dr. Henry Locock, Mayor of Northampton in 1749, had this sloping pavement to the door of his Sheep Street home constructed so that he could step straight into his carriage. The four-windowed room over the porch was called the Observatory and was removed, along with the incline known as Locock's Hill, in 1927. One of Dr. Locock's descendants was *accouchiére* to Queen Victoria, attending the birth of all her children. Later occupants included other doctors, a Vicar of the nearby round Church of the Holy Sepulchre and, during the First World War, the Military.

SHEEP STREET. NORTHAMPTON.

17. Sheep Street, where the sheep market was held for several centuries, pictured during the First World War from the junction with Bearward Street, a thoroughfare named because bear pits were once there and which has totally disappeared in the changes of the 1960s and 1970s. Sheep Street has also been cut into three, with east-west roads being built across the former north-south pattern. This part of the eastern side of the street included the shops of Hamps, furnishers, and Partridge's, clothiers and outfitters.

18. One of the earlier road widening schemes in the town involved the removal of the Prudential Buildings at the junction of St. Giles Street and Derngate. As well as the well-known insurance company, firms occupying the building included solicitors Darnell and Price among the partners of which was 'Pat' Darnell, who continued to dress in Victorian style of top hat and frock coat until his death in 1955, at the age of 90.

19. The Workhouse (left) was a feature of Wellingborough Road before the Second World War. Glimpsed beyond it, at the corner of Market Street, is the Spread Eagle public house, one of the few corner-of-terraced street pubs in Northampton to have a reincarnation. After closure following the demolition of Market Street and other terraced streets between Wellingborough Road and Kettering Road, it seemed certain to follow and was leased to Northampton Men's Own Rugby Club pending demolition. In August 1982, it reopened as a Charles Wells house, with different beer but still retaining the old atmosphere.

20. Market Street's terraced houses disappeared along with those of the parallel Portland Street and Cleveland Road but the next street going out of town, Artizan Road, has survived and looks today much as it did when this picture was taken in Edwardian times. The 'Phipps Ale and Stout' sign is on a corner shop and at the next corner is the Artizan's Arms, which still survives today.

21. On the two town centre ends of Abington Street were C. Holyoak's wine and spirits shop and Spoor and Son, outfitters and tailors. Next to Holyoaks on the Market Square was the Three Tuns Inn. In the first floor window on Spoors' corner old Mrs. Spoor would sit for hour after hour surveying the passing scene. The tram-lines were for horse-trams which were introduced in June 1881, and continued until July 1904.

Abington Street, Northampton

22. The impressive house on the left of Abington Street was once that of Dr. Rae. It was demolished in 1907 and offices for Northampton Gas Company were erected on the site so that, as a local publication put it, 'the public will be saved the dismal experience of wandering about the odiferous regions of Gas Street to pay their bills'. On the site today is Marks and Spencers.

Mare Fair, Northampton

23. The North Western Hotel and other premises on the north side of Marefair have now been replaced by the monolithic Barclaycard building, the national headquarters of the credit card offshoot of the bank. The hotel site was previously occupied by small cottages among which was the Rose and Punchbowle Inn. In 1897 this was rebuilt as the Rose and Punchbowl Hotel which was renamed when purchased by the London and North Western Railway Company. Midway along the other side was Freeschool Street on the corner of which was the Falcon public house, with distinctive caryatids of carved wood supporting the fascia.

24. The corner of Marefair and Horsemarket was the original home of Latimer and Crick, dealers in hay, straw and chaff, founded about 1880. When the premises were pulled down in 1887 the business moved to the former theatre just opposite, on the corner of Marefair and Horseshoe Street. This was in turn demolished in road widening of 1922 and Latimer and Crick moved first to Horsemarket and later to a riverside location on the corner of Bridge Street and Cattle Market Road.

25. 'Good Accommodation for Cyclists' was offered above Propert's Luncheon and Tea Rooms at the corner of Marefair and Chalk Lane.

26. Looking up Gold Street about 1906. This was where the town's first parking restrictions had been introduced in 1849 when the Mayor (Francis Parker) made a regulation that carriers' carts on the south side should range themselves from the Crow and Horseshoe, on the corner with Horseshoe Street, to Hogan's Soda Water Factory while those on the north side should be placed between the Wheatsheaf Inn and the Goat Inn (where the bay windows project on the left). Later, despite this rule, Earl Spencer complained that there was not enough room for his carriage to be driven between the parked lines of vehicles.

27. One of Northampton's pioneer cyclists and motorists was Joseph Grose. In July 1883, he achieved the then surprising speed of nearly 20 miles per hour on Leicester Cycle Track, riding a 52-inch wheeled 'Ordinary'. He was an enthusiast of the Penny Farthing Cycle which he rode with the Northampton Victoria Cycle Club. In the latter part of the 1880s he opened a cycle shop in Horseshoe Street and designed and manufactured his own models. Here are two of them, ridden by Mr. Grose and his wife.

28. Later Joseph Grose moved to the corner of Horseshoe Street and Gold Stgreet, a site where the town's first tavern music hall had operated from 1855. Later the premises returned to an entertainment role, first as the Palace of Varieties and then as the Majestic Cinema, which closed in the 1930s after which the building stood derelict, an eyesore for many years.

29. Northampton's first motor car, a Coventry Motette, is driven by Joseph Grose in Marefair, where the national headquarters of Barclaycard now stand, but then past the Rose and Punchbowle Inn and the shop of fishmonger S. Mudd. This was in 1896. The three-wheel Motette purchased from Mr. McRobbie Turrell, of Coventry, was only the third such vehicle made in England. The driver sat above the engine with the passenger in a sort of armchair in front – a case of back-seat driving! The passenger in the picture was Mr. W.H. Green, known popularly as 'Old Doc Green', an engineer and designer of gas engines. The following year Mr. Grose bought a 3½h.p. Benz chassis on which he built a body of his own design. Today Grose Ltd. is one of the leading garages and car dealers in Northampton.

30. Horse-trams, like this one in Abington Street, began in 1881. The first were single-decked and quite crude. They were operated by Northampton Street Tramways Company whose premises were in Abington Street, where the Public Libraries now stand. The first route was from Castle Station to Kingsley Park Hotel (the Elephant) which was extended after a few months to Cafe Square, St. James. A return trip of the four miles took an hour. The following year the route was further lengthened to Melbourne Gardens, renamed Franklins Gardens in 1887 when they were taken over by John Campbell Franklin. The earlier name was after Lord Melbourne who had an estate at nearby Duston and who was the first Prime Minister and father figure for the youthful Queen Victoria.

31. The inauguration of the electric tram service on 21 July 1904, followed the purchase of the trams by Northampton Corporation. Four decorated cars loaded with guests and councillors left Mercers Row and travelled to Abington Park where tea was provided. This photograph was taken at Abington Park. On the platform are the German-born transport manager, Mr. Julius Gottschalk, and the Mayor (Councillor Edward Lewis). On Saturday 23 July, 27,000 people rode on the trams and on Sunday 24 July, a further 15,000.

32. Celebrating the arrival of the first electric tram at Abington Park Hotel (today known simply as the Abington and brewing some of its own beer). Northampton Corporation had bought the system from Northampton Street Tramways Co. in October 1901, for £37,000. The headquarters were moved from Abington Street to St. James End where the 22 horse-trams, a few horse-buses, and over 100 horses could be better accommodated. In January 1904, work began on the conversion to electric trams. The horse-drawn service to Far Cotton continued for a further decade because of the difficult slope of Bridge Street.

33. Kingsley Park is the destination of the tram on the left of this scene at the lower end of the Drapery – but the advertisement for Fry's Cocoa stands out much more clearly! At the top of the Drapery the demolition of premises for the rounding off of the corner of the Parade and Sheep Street had taken place when this picture was taken but the new buildings had not yet been erected and the props supporting the end building can be seen.

34. View of Gold Street about 1908. The chain horse seen approaching on the right was one of several kept at Castle Station to assist loaded wagons up Black Lion Hill and Gold Street. On the right the former Grose premises, then the Palace of Varieties, which was to be taken over in September 1913, by Leon Vint and known as Vint's Palace. He began with cine-variety. This was eventually the site for many years of the tile and fireplace shop of A. Bell and Co.

35. Along Kingsthorpe Road the tram ran past the Cock Hotel (left). Advertised on the tram in the picture is the Cinema de Luxe, which opened in March 1914, in Campbell Street on the site of the former stables of the Bull Hotel, Regent Square, which was recently demolished for road improvements at this busy junction where the town's north gate was once located. The Cinema de Luxe seated about 1,000 and was run in tandem with the Picturedrome, Kettering Road, opened in November 1912.

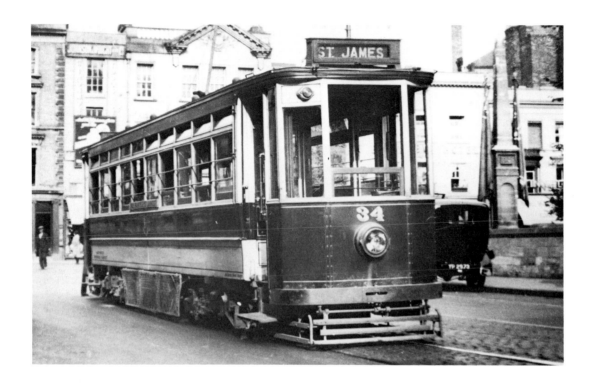

36. On less busy routes and at off-peak times some single-deck trams were operated. Waiting in Mercers Row, about 1925, this one was bound for St. James. Installing the tram lines had been a major operation costing £85,000. Blocks of Norwegian granite were used to pave the area between the rails. Power was originally supplied by burning the town's refuse in special boilers. The 60 navvies employed went on strike for an extra penny an hour on the 5½d they were getting but they were unsuccessful.

37. Driver, conductor and inspector pose for a photograph on car No. 6. At the time of the picture the tram was open fronted with an open upper deck. Later the cars were covered in and three-sided glass screens added to protect the driver. The guard under the car was connected to a switch which cut off the power if it struck an obstruction (such as a pedestrian!). In later years the track became so uneven that the guard would sometimes catch the ground and stop the drive.

38. After trams of the horse-drawn and electric varieties came the buses of which three early examples are seen. The last tram ran in December 1934, but the first buses had appeared in September 1923, with solid tyres for the first four years.

39. The Mayorhold served as an open air bus station for several services as seen in this snapshot loaned by Mrs. Margaret Athas, of Oriskany, New York, who, as Margaret Sherwin, was the last licensee of the Old Jolly Smokers (marked by an arrow) which was on the site of the first Town Hall. Two other public houses stood opposite, the King's Head on the Mayorhold, and the Green Dragon at the end of Bearward Street. Everything seen on this picture has been obliterated by modern redevelopment, except for the ancient Church of the Holy Sepulchre, of which the spire is glimpsed. The name Mayorhold may have derived from the early Town Hall or from a Mare Pound located there.

40. Note the open tops of the two double-deck buses in the Mayorhold. The Old Jolly Smokers is seen on the right, at the top of Scarletwell Street.

41. A char-à-banc outing from the Racehorse Inn on Abington Square. The vehicle was built locally, by Hollingsworths, on a Maudslay chassis, to the special requirements of Mr. Robinson, the landlady of the Racehorse, who ordered it from the Derngate Motor Company in 1911.

42. One of the major acts of vandalism in Victorian Northampton was the removal of the last remains of the Castle to clear a site for Northampton's third railway station, known as Castle Station. This picture was taken in 1875. It is believed that the Castle was erected by Simon de St. Liz (or Senlis), first Earl of Northampton, in about 1084. Thomas à Becket, Archbishop of Canterbury, stood trial there in 1146. Between 1332 and 1333 the deaths of 11 prisoners in its dungeons were attributed by a Coroner's Jury to cold, hunger, thirst and privation. By the beginning of the 14th century it was becoming dilapidated but continued to be used as a gaol. After the Civil War it was partly demolished on the orders of the restored monarch Charles II because the town had supported the Parliamentary cause against his father, Charles I.

43. Built on the site of the former Castle, Castle Station became part of the London, Midland and Scottish Railway until nationalisation after the Second World War. The name board proclaimed: 'Direct Route London and the South, Rugby, Birmingham, Liverpool, Manchester and the North, Market Harborough, Melton Mowbray, Nottingham and Peterborough and East Coast.' When the station opened in 1881 the Northampton Mercury newspaper observed: 'Northampton now becomes a suburb of London. A gentleman who begins business at 10 and finishes at 4 can now run up to town by train, complete his day's work and return to the bosom of his family in time for a fashionable dinner.'

44. The ornate buildings of St. John's Street Station are in the background of this picture of a Royal visit to Northampton. St. John's was one of Northampton's three railway stations. The first was in Bridge Street and followed the beginning of the railways. Opened in June 1845, it operated until 1964 and has been demolished. St. John's came next in June 1872, and lasted until 1939. Finally came the Castle Station, where there had been only a minor halt from 1859.

45. The Diamond Jubilee celebrations of the reign of Queen Victoria in 1897 were marked by many street parties especially in the old 'Borough' area of Northampton between Horsemarket and the Mayorhold and Castle Station. Houses had been crammed into this area, in terraces and courts. This party in St. Andrew's Gardens is said to have consisted of the members of a single family.

46. The proclamation of a new monarch used to take place on the steps of the Market Square Fountain. This was the scene on 10 May 1910, at the Accession of George V. Along with Town Councillors and officials is the Chief Constable, Mr. Fred H. Mardlin, who held office from 1887 to 1923. In 130 years there were only four Chief Constables of the Borough Police Force. The first was Henry Keenan, who took over from Superintendent Joe Ball who had been in charge from the formation in 1829 until 1851. John Williamson was the 'Chief' from 1924 to 1955 when Dennis Baker held the reins until the Borough Force was amalgamated into the County Constabulary in 1966.

CORONATION CELEBRATIONS, NORTHAMPTON. JUNE 1911.

47. As part of the celebrations for the Coronation of George V in June 1911, a 'procession of historical and emblematic cars and military contingents' took place to Abington Park. Scenes on carts included 'Civic Reception for Charles I' by scholars of Military Road School and this one enigmatically entitled: 'When Did You Last See Your Father?' by the Juniors of Stimpson Avenue School. This was taken in Wellingborough Road with the fish shop of F. Tuckley on the corner with Wilby Street.

CORONATION CELEBRATIONS, NORTHAMPTON. JUNE 1911.

48. A service of praise was held on the Market Square to mark the Coronation of George V in June 1911. Northampton Musical Society took part along with several choirs, the conducting being shared between Mr. C.J. King, conductor of the Society, Mr. Brook Sampson, who ran a music school in Beethoven House, the Georgian building next to the gabled Welsh House at the bottom of Newland, and Councillor Joseph Rogers, the Town Councillor who was largely responsible for inaugurating band concerts in Abington Park. The Mayor (Councillor S. Yarde), who called for three cheers for the King, had given £50 towards the fund launched to pay for the celebrations, which raised £1,462. There was also a balance of 13s 6d from the 1902 Coronation celebrations fund.

49. Two years later the townsfolk had the opportunity to see their new monarch in person. George V and Queen Mary were welcomed on the Market Square by the Mayor (Councillor Harvey Reeves), who was accustomed to playing a leading role. For many years he was a prominent member of Northampton Amateur Operatic Company which presented annual musicals, first in the Opera House (now Royal Theatre) where he was Pooh-Bah in 'The Mikado' in 1899, and from 1922 at the New Theatre. In the first show there, immediately following his second Mayoralty, he played the Baillie in 'Les Cloches de Corneville'.

50. In a speech which was totally inaudible except to those close at hand (no amplification systems then!) the King said: 'It gives me great pleasure that by my attending the military manoeuvres in this district an opportunity has been given to us to come amongst you and renew for the first time since the visit of Queen Victoria in 1844 that long connection between Northampton and the Throne.' Every time the King mentioned the name of Northampton the Mayor gave a courtly bow. The route from Northampton to the home of Earl Spencer, at Althorp, was arranged to pass the bust of the King's late father, Edward VII, outside Northampton General Hospital. The King saluted as his car drove slowly past. Earl Spencer is on the right of the group on the dais, erected in front of the Parade side of the Market Square.

51. Councillors, officials and their ladies were seated before the dais for the 1913 Royal visit. Many thousands of citizens stood behind them for the 15 minute visit. The Band of the Lifeguards played from the steps of the Fountain.

52. Veterans of the Indian Mutiny and Crimean War watched from in front of Abels music shop, including Col. Campbell, of Salcey Lawn, a former aide-de-camp to the King, and Mrs. Mason, centre, widow of one of the noble six hundred who rode into the valley of death in the Charge of the Light Brigade, at the Battle of Balaclava.

53. The first seven years of George Warwick's half-century in the chimney business were spent as a climber. He was only 11 when he began, in 1873, getting up at three o'clock in the morning to go up such chimneys as those of Northampton's George and Angel Hotels and of the Corn Exchange. He told a reporter that he rarely fell during those ascents as 'the chimneys were none too wide even for such a little fellow as I was and by sticking out my legs and elbows I could stop myself'. In the county his calls included Brixworth Hall (now demolished) and Holdenby House. As a rule he did not finish until 9.30 or 10 at night, after which he slept in the sweep's cellar. Later he set up on his own.

54. This horse-drawn delivery cart is seen outside W. Hewitt's grocery shop at the lower end of a row of cottages in Wood Street. On the left of the shop is a jetty in the rear of houses in Princes Street. The site is now buried below the Grosvenor Centre, almost opposite where the Job Centre stands today, the only surviving building from the old street pattern.

55. The postman with his pony and trap is in Dychurch Lane at the rear of the Post Office in Abington Street. Erected in 1872 this was the first Government Post Office in the town, built as a result of the Telegraph Act of 1868 which took the telegraph service out of private hands. Northampton's first Post Office was for a century at the bottom of the Drapery, combined with a printing and bookselling establishment. The first postmaster was Mr. J. Lacy and there were only six postmasters in 150 years, his successors being Mr. R. Birdsall and Mr. George Wetton (who produced a notable directory of the town). A new site was acquired in 1910 in St. Giles Street, between Mr. Whitton's lastmaking works and the St. Giles Dairy but the new premises were not erected until 1917. Photo by H.J. Leeson, Hood Street.

56. There were many diverse businesses in the Mayorhold and Horsemarket, which led south from it towards the junction with Gold Street and Marefair. At No. 70 Horsemarket Mr. C. Warren was licensed to sell cigarettes as the sign on his window proclaimed and the brands he stocked included Wills Woodbines and Park Drive, as shown in the projecting signs. But he sold many other general items and various directories of the late 1920s and 1930s list him as a fruiterer and wholesale potato merchant and retail grocer.

57. Hats and hosiery formed the main business of Hollis and Co. in their new premises following the rounding-off of the corner of the Parade with Sheep Street. The firm was at one time in Gold Street, 'Hollis, Hatters' being listed there in the 1845 Directory. Shops like this are few and far between now. As Grace Nicholls wrote in a poem called 'Change' in the 1970s: *Shops I knew half a century ago/ have changed or gone, ousted by chain stores/ or the Centre, that multi-million show./ Strident chrome, tiles and shatterproof glass/ glisten in the unwonted sunless heat/ fluorescent lights switch on the days/ masking time and season by deceit.*

58. Another shop, this one with a particularly ornate frontage, which lost its original premises was Phillips with 'Linens, Flannels, Blankets, Carpets, Dress Goods and Hosiery', as this picture of about 1900 shows. The firm had been started in a first floor room in Dychurch Lane in 1886 by Mr. A. Phillips, a retired commercial traveller who moved here from Newark to set his three sons up in business. The move to Abington Street came in 1898 but the premises shown were erected the following year to the design of a Scottish architect, A.E. Anderson. In 1972 the firm moved to Abington Square and York Road and the Abington Street buildings were demolished to make way for a shopping scheme funded by the Prudential Assurance Company.

59. This remarkable display of poultry and game was mounted by F.H. Phillips and Co. whose shop was between the entrance to the George Hotel Mews and and the Coach and Horses public house in George Row. The firm had a wholesale fish merchants business in Newcastle on Tyne and North Shields and owned steam fishing vessels. The establishment at 2 George Row had been founded by Mr. John Clark in 1836 and was subsequently run by a Mr. Brown before being taken over by Phillips who adopted the telegraphic address of 'Goldfish, Northampton'. In season they offered salmon, soles, brill, sturgeon, John Dories, turbot, halibut, cod, ling, whitebait, smelts, herrings, haddock, whitings, skate, mackerel, plaice, flounders, red mullet, grey mullet, eels, gurnets, lobsters, crabs, prawns, shrimps, native and sauce oysters, bloaters, kippers, Finnan haddock, sprats, salt fish, etc. They offered a delivery service to customers' homes.

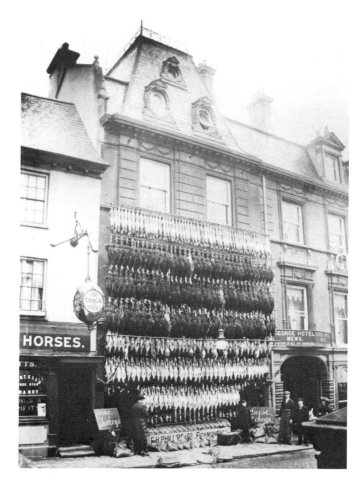

60. Totally vanished is the line of shops and public houses on the east side of Kettering Road as far as the former Market Street. The Queen's Arms, the Raglan Arms, the Cleveland Arms and the New Inn vanished along with the terraced streets between Kettering Road and Wellingborough Road – Cleveland Road, Raglan Street and Portland Street. For many years these corner premises with Cleveland Road had been occupied by A. Watts and Son, 'the leading furnishers in the Midlands,' which had been set up in Adnitt Road about 1895 selling mangles, mail-carts (a light vehicle to carry children) and bassinets (a wickerwork cradle or perambulator). In the 1920s Watts moved to purpose-built premises in Abington Street, where they still remain as one of the few local firms. The premises shown were later used by another furnishers, Parsonson Bros. Ltd., now at 201, Wellingborough Road on the site of a former monumental masons' yard.

61. The expansion of Northampton during the past century has brought an increase in population from 53,000 (1884) to 165,000 (1984) and involved the absorption of several villages – Kingsthorpe, Abington, Dallington, Weston Favell, Great Houghton, Great Billing, Little Billing, Hardingstone, Wootton, Collingtree and Duston, pictured here in the old days. It fought twice to prevent being taken in but eventually failed, in 1965.

DALLINGTON, NORTHAMPTON.

62. This village green picture was taken in the early 1900s at Dallington, which was absorbed in 1932. Although covered by a Conservation order it is hemmed in by council estates at Kings Heath and Spencer and in 1977 the then vicar, the Reverend John Clarkson, stated: 'The central community life of the area has been destroyed. It is not easy for the people of Dallington to feel that they belong to each other.' Buildings on Smarts Farm, formerly Old Dairy Farm, have been turned into houses so that some Dallingtonians of the 1980s live in former cowsheds!

63. Just round the corner from the previous picture is this one of the 1890s by Henry Cooper showing the alsmhouses built by Sir Richard Raynsford in 1673 and restored in 1957. The village school, today no longer in use as such, had yet to be built, to the right of the almshouses, when this picture was taken. In 1983 the village acquired a much-desired bypass when a new major highway was opened between Weedon Road and Harborough Road. Dallington Hall (not pictured) was in the possession of the Earl Spencers before being turned into a convalescent home. Lately it has been sub-divided and a major portion is occupied by Mr. Robert Spencer, a cousin of the Princess of Wales.

64. Floods like these at Victoria Promenade, near the Cattle Market, were not uncommon in the town in former times. In 1880 a man delivering coal by horse and cart at St. James was swept away in 10 feet of water and drowned. In February 1939, the worst inundations for thirty years occurred. In 1970 Abington Park Lake became blocked and Abington Park Hotel had 10 inches of water in its cellars.

65. Mill Lane was the country lane which led down from Kingsthorpe to the mill on the River Nene. This scene of the 1880s did not change a great deal until the 1970s and continued to lead its narrow way round sharp bends round the mill site and over the railway line. Then the new major highway from Harborough Road was begun. There are now houses on either side of the former rural scene.

Hunsbury Hill Furnaces, Northampton.

66. Perched on a site overlooking the town Hunsbury Hill Furnaces closed in 1921, although the chimney was not knocked down until 1949. Excavations have revealed the remains of a Roman villa but the site is believed to go back to the Iron Age. This history is being researched by members of Northamptonshire Ironstone Railway Trust who operate a passenger carrying railway service in the 82 acre Country Park which has been created as part of the southern expansion of the town.

Wootton Windmill

67. One of thousands of windmills that used to operate in England was this one at Wootton which was in use until 1914. For 700 years windmills ground grain and powered light industry. This tower one at Wootton was similar to many in Northamptonshire including those at Blakesley, Whiston, Brixworth and Stoke Bruerne. One in Market Street, Northampton, survived until the 1870s. During the Second World War the windmill pictured served as an observation post for the Home Guard. The field in which it stood was where the Parliamentary forces under Fairfax were camped during the Civil War. Today, shorn of several feet of its height, the one-time mill has been turned into a garden house in the grounds of Windmill House, built for Mr. Denis Bell in 1952.

Kingsthorpe
High Street

68. Kingsthorpe village was absorbed into the Borough in 1900 but with the aid of its cul-de-sac situation and a Conservation order it has been able to preserve much of its former character. This postcard dating from about 1904 is of the village High Street. Kingsthorpe got its name because the Manor of Thorpe was held by King William (the Conqueror). It housed people who worked on the Royal estates at Moulton Park, now a vast industrial and business estate. King John leased it to the people.

69. After standing derelict for many years the site of the former Horseshoe Inn on the Wellingborough Road at Weston Favell has recently become a housing area. As recently as 1926 a Town Guide stated: 'The village is about 2¼ miles east of the town.' It is now well within the Borough, much of the recent expansion having been to the east, reaching out nearly to the village of Ecton, once regarded as half-way between Northampton and Wellingborough.

Tower & Recreation Room, War Hospital, Duston.

70. Built in 1876 as the County Lunatic Asylum and now known as St. Crispin's Hospital (but still for mental patients) these buildings became a War Hospital during the First World War. Servicemen are seen taking the air in front of the tower and recreation room. In its old guise as a lunatic asylum it was known popularly as Berrywood and harassed mothers would tell their naughty children: 'You'll send me to Berrywood!' Until the opening of St. Andrew's Hospital (now the country's largest private mental hospital) as Northampton Lunatic Asylum in 1838 lunatics had been kept in the Town Gaol in Fish Street, chained to the floor and lying on beds of straw.

71. The staffs of the Registrar, Quarter-Master, and Dispenser at the 'War Hospital', Duston, are included in this group. Note the lengths of the skirts of the women's uniforms.

72. Manfield Hospital was given to the town at the suggestion of a Northampton journalist. As Weston Favell House, it had been the home of shoe manufacturer James Manfield, who put it on the market in 1923. When it did not sell Mr. W.H. Holloway, founder and editor of the Northampton Independent, wrote an article saying that it would make an ideal hospital for crippled children... 'We are assured that 90 per cent of these afflicted little ones could be cured.' This was read by Mr. Manfield, then in Italy, who cabled his secretary, H.G. Lewis, to offer it. Sadly Mr. Manfield did not live to see it opened, in 1925. It is now part of the National Health Service and in its grounds is the Cynthia Spencer House, mainly for cancer patients, named in memory of Countess Spencer and opened by her great friend the Queen Mother in May, 1976. Her Majesty was accompanied by the 14-year-old Lady Diana Spencer who returned as Princess of Wales in March, 1985, to open an adjacent day clinic.

73. Scarcely a head without a hat as a Food Proclamation was read by the Mayor (Councillor John Woods) at Northampton Guild (or Town) Hall in May, 1917. The Proclamation was by the King and asked people to cut down on bread by at least a quarter. Erected in 1864 to the design of E.W. Godwin the Town Hall replaced a castellated one at the corner of Abington Street and Wood Hill. It was extended in 1892. The hall gave its name to Guildhall Road, just opposite, which was built about the same time and which is by far the youngest street in the town centre.

74. Field guns on parade on the Market Square during the First World War. After the war the town acquired a tank which was placed in Abington Park where it became a subject of pacifist and aesthetic controversy. It made its way from Castle Station to Abington Park under its own power and took two days to do so, as it broke down twice en route. It was a 'male' tank, with cannons in the turrets as opposed to mere machine guns on the tanks of the opposite gender.

75. During the petrol shortages of the two wars, 1914-1918 and 1939-1945, some vehicles used gas as a means of propulsion, the gaseous fuel being stored in a bag atop the vehicle. Gas conversion first came to Northampton in 1917, using coal gas drawn from the town supply, a tube taking the gas into the air intake of the carburetor. Gas was used for Beeden's buses including the one pictured on the Northampton-Towcester route; also by the Midland Motor Bus Company, later known as the Midland Red.

76. Gas also propelled vans. This converted 12 h.p. delivery van was used by the Electric Laundry in Hood Street. The firm calculated that the gas cost the equivalent of petrol at 6d a gallon. The unladen weight of the van was 12 cwt. while fully loaded it was 18 cwt. and could be driven 22 miles on a full gas bag of 140 cubic feet, costing 4½d.

77. A Northampton shop which was 'To Let' was pressed into service as a Navy Recruiting Office during the First World War. Note the preponderance of caps worn by the new recruits about to enter the service.

78. The East End Bantam Fusiliers was the name adopted by this group of children from East Street, a terraced street leading off Wellingborough Road. Before the First World War they had been the 'East Street Gang' but after the conflict broke out they taught themselves to march and drill, buying odd items of uniform and carving wooden 'rifles'. The E.E.B.F. visited other areas in the town and also nearby villages giving drill displays and collecting money and gifts for wounded soldiers in local hospitals.

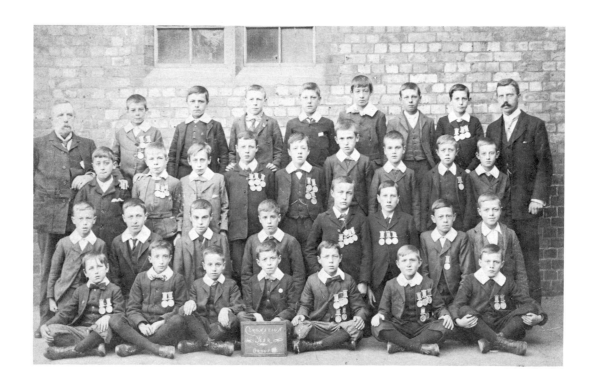

79. Bemedalled boys at Kettering Road Board School probably taken at the time of the Coronation of Edward VII in 1902. One of the medals is that presented to all schoolchildren in the Borough. The others are probably for good attendance.

80. A class at Barry Road Infants School about 1908. The brown glazed bricks are very distinctive and have changed little over the years. The school was opened in 1901 with Mr. F.E. Harris, a noted disciplinarian, as headmaster. The following year saw the inauguration of the school swimming baths where tens of thousands of children from many schools learned to swim.

81. Several much-loved members of the staff of Northampton Grammar School (also known as the Town and County School) appear in this group taken on the steps to the main entrance. Second from left is the Borough's Chief Education Officer, Mr. H.C. Perrin; the tall man next to him is Education Committee Chairman Councillor W.H. Percival; then Mr. Ben Swinden and the Headmaster Mr. W.C.C. Cooke. On right is Councillor C.N.J. Butterfield, proprietor of the Northampton Daily Chronicle, and next to him Canon J. Trevor Lewis, vicar of All Saints Church. Teachers in the rear row, on the right of Mr. Cooke, are Mr. A.M. Walmsley, Dr. E.E. Field (deputy headmaster, known universally as 'Gus'), and 'Taffy' Davies. The school had moved from Abington Square to Billing Road in 1911.

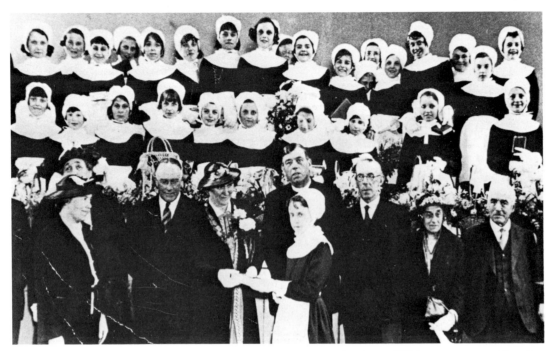

82. Before the introduction of compulsory State education in 1870 the town was served by private and charity schools among which were the Blue Coat and Orange School for boys and the Beckett and Sargeant School for girls, both of which had their entrances in Kingswell Street, although the premises of the former were in Bridge Street (and survive today as a Leather Museum). Both had colourful uniforms. Summer dress for the girls included bonnet, tippet (cape) and apron. Everything that could be starched was! Winter dress included a long, thick brown cloak. The school was started in 1735 by two spinsters, Dorothy Beckett and Anne Sargeant, with the aim of teaching girls to run a home in a clean and orderly manner. Attendance at All Saints Church on Sundays was compulsory. The school did not close until 1962 and some of its traditions are carried on at All Saints Middle School, Boughton Green Road. The clergyman in this 1930s picture is Canon J. Trevor Lewis, vicar of All Saints.

The Dining Hall
Convent of Notre Dame
Northampton

83. This was the dining room of Notre Dame High School which stood in Abington Street from 1879 to 1975. In 1845 three nuns of the Congregation of the Infant Jesus of Nivelles, Belgium, had set up a small community in Sheep Street and taught in local day and Sunday schools, also taking poor children in their own workroom. Later they moved to a building which formed part of the church which preceded the present Roman Catholic Cathedral in Barrack Road. It was in 1851 that three houses were acquired in Abington Street. After an outbreak of typhus this community dispersed but nuns from the Notre Dame order took over in 1852. After pupils moved out to the new Thomas Becket Upper School in the 1970s the buildings were sold and demolished to make way for shops and offices.

The above Group represents a gathering of the Recipients and Workers of the

❧ ❧ FREE BREAKFAST, ❧ ❧

at the Salvation Army Barracks, Guildhall Road, Northampton, 1905.

84. A free breakfast was given for the poor of Northampton in 1905 at the Salvation Army Barracks in Guildhall Road. 'Army' occasions were frequently the target of attacks by hooligans, especially the 1882 visit of General Booth when there was a near riot and the instruments of the marching band were seized and smashed up. When the mob made for the carriage in which General Booth was travelling he was protected by his son who was told by his father: 'You will live to come to Northampton and be welcomed in these very streets.' This prophecy came true when the son, then General Booth, came to town in 1927 to open a new Salvation Army Hall in Brunswick Place, off Kettering Road. That hall was demolished in the 1970s.

85. The gateway to the bottled beer store of Whitbread and Co. in Newland later became the factory entrance to the Lotus shoe factory. In this picture of about 1908 workmen are relaying the road surface with the aid of an Allchin steam-roller which had been made at South Bridge. Today this section of Newland is the only piece remaining identifiable although all the buildings have gone and new offices are being erected. The rest of the ancient thoroughfare disappeared with the construction of the Grosvenor Centre.

86. An oriel window was a feature of the New York Tavern which was in Horsemarket. Why New York? No-one seems to know. The drawing was done by T. Osborne Robinson shortly before the pub was demolished, being among dozens which closed during the twenty years after the Second World War. This one was owned by Phipps Brewery which had been founded by Pickering Phipps at Towcester in 1801 and moved to Northampton's Bridge Street, near the River Nene, in 1817. From 1856 its next door neighbour was its arch rival, first called the Phoenix Brewery, then the Steam Brewery and later operated by Northampton Brewery Company. Phipps and N.B.C. merged in 1957, as Phipps Northampton Brewery Co. Ltd.

87. The Horse and Jockey public house was on the corner of Lady's Lane and Park Street. The poster on the wall dates the picture as it advertises a play at the Opera House (now Royal Theatre) during the week commencing 20 May 1907 – 'Her Love Against the World' by Walter Howard. The Horse and Jockey belonged to Northampton Brewery Company.

BENTLEY'S

15 LOFTY BEDROOMS!

STABLING FOR 60 HORSES!

CONCERT HALL

PALACE OF AMUSEMENT!

CROSS KEYS HOTEL,

SHEEP STREET, NORTHAMPTON.

88. Bentley's, in Sheep Street, was one of a number of taverns which provided entertainment. Bentley was the name of the proprietor, the tavern being the Cross Keys, which was on the site now occupied by a multi-storey car park. In 1879 there was a free concert every Monday, Wednesday, Thursday and Saturday – when there was a 'first class entertainment comprising vocal and instrumental music of a very superior order, both as regards quality and execution, together with special readings from the standard authors making on the whole an intellectual MELANGE'!

89. Cobbled Marefair (foreground) and Gold Street (narrower, in background) pictured after Leon Vint had taken over the Palace of Varieties in 1913. Glimpsed on the opposite corner, on the right, is the former theatre which served the town from 1806 to 1884, by then converted to shop use. Photo by Henry Cooper.

90. 'Ye Olde Playhouse' on the Marefair portal of Latimer and Crick, corn and seed merchants, recalled the fact that this was the former theatre, which had been a venue for such visiting companies as Robertson's Lincoln Company, Mr. Mudie's Company from the Theatre Royal, Windsor, and Henry Jackman's Company which appeared from 1839 to 1862. In 1884 the theatrical glory faded with the opening of the present theatre in Guildhall Road and these premises were at first used as a Church Army headquarters. The building was demolished in a road widening scheme of 1922. Glimpsed on the right is the Shakespeare Inn which survived until a further road widening of 1974.

91. The 'New Theatre Royal and Opera House', built on an L-shaped site in Guildhall Road, was opened in May 1884. This was the name on the bills but the one engraved in stone on the frontage is 'Royal Theatre and Opera House'. By the appelation derived from this it is now the only 'Royal Theatre' in the world and calls itself by that proud name, especially since visits by the Queen and Princess Anne and by Princess Alexandra, who attended the Centenary performance of 'Great Expectations'. From 1884 to 1927, however, in popular parlance it was known only as the Opera House or 'The Op.'. In 1927 it became Northampton Repertory Theatre, which was shortened to 'The Rep.'. Meantime, in 1925, it had been acquired by Northampton Theatre Syndicate who also owned the rival New Theatre and it was they who let it to the new 'Rep.' company in 1927.

92. Three years after the opening of the Opera House a fire occurred when the 'Jim the Penman' company had moved out following the Saturday night performance which had ended at 10.35 on 12 February 1887. The outbreak was discovered by Arthur Hall, the company's assistant stage manager and baggage man, as he made his way back to his lodgings in Cow Lane, at the rear of the theatre after taking the company gear to the nearby St. John's Street Station. The roof over the stage fell in and flames licked out to consume several rows of seats along with instruments which had been left in the orchestra pit. The theatre was back in business after ten weeks.

93. In 1909 the pit band at the Opera House went on strike for 23 weeks in an effort to get better pay. Joint own-ers of the theatre at the time were Milton Bode and Edward Compton, actor manager and father of Fay Compton, and Compton Mackenzie. By the end of the dispute many of the bandsmen had got jobs at the Castle Roller Skating Rink and only one was re-employed. The stoppage, which was unsuccessful, was part of a coun-try-wide drive for better pay in the pit.

94. We have to step outside the time-span of this collection of 1880-1930 pictures for this one of the unique stage door of the Royal Theatre/Repertory Theatre/Opera House. It is unique because it was on the opposite side of Swan Street from the rear of the theatre. This thoroughfare was originally called Cow Lane because people had driven cattle down it to Cow Meadow. The name was altered in 1890. Today the section of street seen here has mostly been covered by the erection of the Derngate multi-form auditorium next door to the theatre, with doors linking the two buildings erected a century apart.

NORTHAMPTON REPERTORY PLAYERS

95. Operating without a break since 1927 the Northampton Repertory Players are now the longest continuously running repertory theatre in the world. Its formation represented another success for the Northampton Independent which set the ball rolling with an article in 1926 headed: 'Can Northampton establish its own repertory theatre?' This group of 1932 includes some of the players who endeared themselves to the regular playgoers with a very wide selection of plays, initially performed weekly and twice-nightly. In the front row are Sheila Millar, Lala Lloyd, Lois Obee (later known as Sonia Dresdel), Robert Young (producer), Joan Kemp-Welch, Jane Tann, Oswald Dale Roberts, Doreen Morton; rear row, Eric Phillips, Stringer Davis, Osborne Robinson (scenic designer), Noel Howlett, Peppino Santangelo (business manager), Herbert Bradford, Donald Gordon, Peter Rosser and Fred Pratt (carpenter).

96. Osborne Robinson joined Northampton Repertory Company in 1928 and carried on designing and painting sets until shortly before his death in January 1976. At work with him in the paint shop are (left) Keith Lyon and John Piper. Next door to the paint shop was a slaughter-house and the artist recalled: 'Animals used to be driven down the street. You could hear them and the smell would ooze up through the sewers. One day sheep and bullocks charged through the door and trampled a three piece suite.' Most of his output was painted over as soon as the play had ended its run but he has a permanent memorial in the set of panels based on Northampton history in the Grosvenor Centre, viewed by thousands each week.

97. A pierrot troupe called Grapho's Jovial Jollies used to perform on land adjacent to Abington Park. This picture was taken in 1906, the roads seen being Ardington Road and Christchurch Road. In the background are the first houses on the Queen Alexandra estate, which was to include King Edward Road. In 1909 a craze for roller skating led to three rinks being erected within the space of two months, including the American Rink not far from Grapho's enclosure. Within a year the craze had faded somewhat and the rink closed, to be reopened as Grapho's Winter Gardens, with variety and picture shows as well as skating. In March, 1914, the building was destroyed by fire.

98. Bert Grapho (front centre) was the inspiration of the 'Jovial Jollies' Concert Party. Grapho had been a member of the Mulvanas Minstrels in which Billy Jackson was the pianist. When they broke up Grapho and Jackson formed the Jovial Jollies. On tour during the winter they played at Dumbarton where Bert and his wife adopted a nine-year-old boy performer named Wee Jack, who became popular. Bert died about 1930 but his wife, known as 'Mrs. Bert', carried on with Jack until the outbreak of war in 1939. After his adopted mother's death Jack Grapho continued as an entertainer in London until his death in 1970.

99. It was not only for the sale of corn that the vast Corn Exchange, in the Parade, was intended. The prospectus of 1848 said that it would be for 'public meetings, lectures and concerts on a large scale and will provide rooms for literary and other societies'. The main room was called the Music Hall but following a concert in December 1862, the Northampton Mercury newspaper commented: 'The hall was not well filled. Something was lost by those present for unless the hall is well-filled the resonance is intolerable. We must renew our protest against the obstinate folly of omitting footlights thus presenting the performers as so many silhouettes.' The place was also difficult to heat: at one stage stoves were installed with the chimney pipes stuck out of the windows. Nevertheless when Mr. D'Oyly Carte sent an opera company to the town in 1882 to perform Gilbert and Sullivan's 'Patience', then still running at the Savoy, London, they played at the Exchange rather than at the diminutive theatre in Marefair. Fanny Kemble gave Shakespearian readings there in 1854 and Jenny Lind sang in 1862. But the event pictured is a bird show.

MEMBERS of Northampton Musical Society and guest soloists at a performance of Bach's Mass in B Minor given at the Exchange Cinema in the thirties. The conductor was Mr. C. J. King, who was organist at St. Matthew's and music master at Northampton Grammar School.

100. For decades there were intermittent campaigns for a proper concert hall and nowadays concerts are among the many types of events at the multi-form Derngate centre. But during the 1930s the Exchange Cinema, a conversion from the Corn Exchange into a cinema in 1920, was among the concert venues. In December 1930, Northampton Musical Society and guest soloists are pictured at a performance of Bach's Mass in B Minor conducted by Mr. C.J. King, organist at St. Matthew's Church and music master at Northampton Grammar School. Talkies had arrived in August 1929; the name changed to the Gaumont in 1950 and Odeon in 1964 until closure as a cinema in 1974. Since then it has been used for bingo.

101. This Cycle Parade in 1912 was the 22nd such event in the town having begun in 1890. In this picture the Delhi Durbar of George V of 1911 was portrayed by the Rover Cycling Club in conjunction with the 16th Lancers. The float in the background depicted the Royal dais with the King and Queen. The entry took first prize in the club class.

102. Although it was a Cycle Parade a donkey-drawn cart with a Pearly King in charge was eligible. The photograph was taken by W.J. Mead of Lady's Lane.

103. This is a picture of the Northampton picture house that never was! The plan was to build it on the site of the then George Hotel, at the corner of George Row and Bridge Street. It was to have been the town's largest cinema, with no fewer than 2,600 seats. The Town Council refused the application and also tried to halt the erection of the Coliseum Cinema, in the belief that housing for returning ex-soldiers was more important in 1919.

THE THEATRE, NORTHAMPTON

104. Significant competition for the Opera House came with the opening in December 1912, of the New Theatre in Abington Street, which was over twice the size. It became a venue for musicals, concerts, ballet, opera and many other forms of entertainment in addition to its staple fare of variety. It had periods of great prosperity during the two world wars but suffered from the competition of films, especially after the advent of 'talkies' and from television in the late 1940s. It closed in 1958 after a succession of nude shows, including the last 'Strip! Strip! Hooray!' and was demolished in 1960.

105. On the principle of 'If you can't beat them, join them' the New Theatre itself became a cinema for a time in 1933. Unlike the other nine cinemas then operating, the Picturedrome, Exchange, Cinema de Luxe, Coliseum, Majestic, Temperance Hall, Regal, Plaza and St. James Cinema (later Roxy), it used back projection, with the film projector behind the screen operating through a hole in the backstage wall. Stage shows returned the following year but meantime Norman Malcom and His Mayfair Broadcasting Orchestra were brought in to play on the stage, later reverting to the pit. One week in 1935 the bandleader disappeared with the band's pay but the players remained, some until the theatre closed.

106. There had been dancing for the general populace of Northampton since Victorian times, including 'Dancing for the Million' at the Corn Exchange but it was in the 1920s that the pastime came into its own at the Salon, Franklin's Gardens, where Brewsters Dance Orchestra, led by Dick Brewster at the piano, is pictured. In 1934 world dancing champion Victor Sylvester wrote: 'Dick Brewster and his band played for our demonstration... his rhythm and tempi were very good indeed... I only wish that every band were up to his standard.' In the 1950s Victor Sylvester returned with his own band, opposite the local band of Art Lewis.

107. Young soccer enthusiasts in 1905 when Northampton Town Boys played Leicester Boys. The photo was sent in 1965 by a Northamptonian living in British Columbia who said that his brother Harry Farmer is seen by the post on the right. He too had emigrated to Canada.

4th Northampton Comp. B.B.Band 1932

108. As well as providing them with healthy outdoor activity the Boys Brigade gave many youngsters a chance to learn musical instruments. This 1932 picture is of the Band of the 4th Northampton Company, founded in 1903. The Northampton Battalion was founded in 1883. The musical tradition continues and in October 1983, the Band of the Duston-based 11th Company, then celebrating its diamond jubilee, led a National Parade in London, with a review at Guildhall by the Lord Mayor.

109. Among the founders of the Northampton Repertory Theatre in 1927 was Alderman W.J. Bassett-Lowke, a member of the famous firm of makers of models of trains, ships etc. George Bernard Shaw (left) visited his Derngate home in 1922 while on a speaking engagement in support of Margaret Bondfield, who was to become the first woman Cabinet Minister. Shaw's play 'Captain Brassbound's Conversion' had mystified local audiences when Ellen Terry appeared in it at the Opera House in 1908. Later Bassett-Lowke built his celebrated modernistic house in Wellingborough Road, called New Ways.

110. This boat house at South Bridge was demolished when the bridge was widened in 1912. On the far side of Bridge Street is the Crown and Anchor pub, once one of some forty licensed premises in that thoroughfare.

111. Boating in Midsummer Meadow, between Rush Mills and Nunn Mills, on the River Nene. The chimney is of Rush Mills, where paper for the original Penny Black postage stamps was made after the introduction of penny post early in the reign of Queen Victoria.

112. Sylvan scene in Abington Park which was given to the town in 1892 by Lady Wantage and opened to the public five years later. The Manor House, known as Abington Abbey, was once the home of Shakespeare's last descendant. The Bard's favourite daughter Elizabeth married Thomas Nash of Welcombe, Warwickshire, and when he died married Sir John Bernard (or Barnard) in 1649 and they lived at the Abbey which had been the home of his family for two centuries. She died in 1669 and was buried in the church.

113. This was the old footpath from Abington Fish Pond to Weston Favell, then a village but now well inside the Borough boundary. The photograph was taken before 1892 when what is now Abington Park was given to the town by Lady Wantage. Was this part of the route of 1780 when Northampton Association for the Prosecution of Felons was concerned with the problems caused by people who were 'breaking down the stiles and gates between Northampton and Abington and Weston Favell'?

(Nº12)

CORONATION CELEBRATIONS, NORTHAMPTON. JUNE 1911.

114. Some 20,000 children marched with bands to the Racecourse for the Coronation celebrations of 1911. In 'the hollow surrounding the spring a large amphitheatre had been railed off and 20,000 young voices were raised in hymns and the National Anthem'. It was a spectacular scene as the children waved leaflets in the colours of red, white and blue. At night there was a firework display at Cow Meadow with 18 illuminated boats and the Town Hall was lit with 1,000 fairy lights.

115. Long before Trinity Avenue was built Seaby's Footpath led from the edge of the Racecourse to join up with Gypsy Lane (now Kingsley Road) near where the Romany public house now stands. This now faded snapshot was taken in January 1875.

116. A top-hatted Victorian takes the air on a seat in Victoria Promenade looking towards Cow Meadow (now re-named Becket's Park) and the River Nene. Cow Meadow was so named because cows were grazed there for centuries, many of them driven down Cow Lane, which was renamed Swan Street in 1890. Before being taken over by Northampton Corporation in 1882 the area was common land and posters in the town offered rewards for anyone who apprehended people, illegally milking the cows grazing there.

117. King John is recorded as buying a pair of boots in Northampton and the town supplied boots for Cromwell's Army during the Civil War. At first the shoemakers worked in their own homes but the mid-Victorian period saw them being enticed to work in factories. The first shoe factory in the town is said to have been this one in Wellington Street, on part of the present site of Marks and Spencers.

118. Mr. William Barratt is pictured with his Morris car outside the Footshape Works of W. Barratt and Co. Ltd. in Kingsthorpe Road of which the architect was A.E. Anderson. Mr. Barratt was the founder of the firm which began in the Drapery and ran a 'Boots by Post' service in which customers were invited to trace the shape of their feet on paper and order by mail – hence 'Footshape'. The car was the Morris Big Six, which was that company's only attempt to break into the big car market. The model was withdrawn after complaints by Rolls Royce as it looked so similar to their cars. In 1936 William Barratt gave the Barratt Maternity Home, Cheyne Walk, to the town.

119. Many women were among the work forces of the shoe factories of the town, being especially employed in the operation called 'closing'. In the rear of this picture at the Barratt factory is the 'Clicking' Room where the leather uppers were cut. The photo was taken following the opening of extensions built by the local firm of Glenn.

120. Workers streaming out of the Footshape shoe factory with many of the men sporting caps, two with trilbies and one with a bowler. Bicycles were the main form of transport, apart from Shanks' Pony (i.e. on foot). The workers are emerging from a new entrance and exit into a large yard which had covered cycle racks and led into Monarch Road. It was a sign of improved living standards after the Second World War when the cycle racks were removed to make way for a car park. There were many redundancies after the firm was taken over by Stylo Shoes of Leeds in 1964 and it was revealed that the firm had lost nearly £1½m in 15 months.

121. Northampton Electric Light and Power Co. Ltd. was inaugurated in 1889 with a capital of £20,000. The first supply to premises in the Town Centre started in March, 1891, with Direct Current. The week's coal was delivered by horse-drawn carts. Those were the days of blue flashes as the old knife switches were opened and closed. This group is of pioneer members of the staff standing by the early generating equipment.

122. The Masonic Hall which served Freemasonry from 1890 to 1972, was in Princes Street, now beneath the site of the Grosvenor Centre. One of the first buildings to be lit by electricity it had been built by Thomas Phipps Dorman, who owned the Opera House and became chairman of the Masonic Hall Company. The hall replaced one in Abington Street and was opened by the Earl of Euston, Provincial Grand Master. When the building was demolished panelling and stained glass depicting the arms of the Earl were removed for installation in the new Masonic Hall in St. George's Avenue.

123. The Northampton Police Force of about 1840. Police estimates featured in the first budget of the Borough Finance Committee, set up in May 1836, allowing for one Superintendent at £1 10s a week, 12 night constables at 14s a week for six months, and 12 night constables at 12s a week for six months. At this time there was no police presence in the daytime. Shortly afterwards it was agreed that there should be day police on Market and Fair Days. Organised beats were established in 1848. The first Police Station was in Derngate, nearly opposite Hazelwood Road, with Superintendent Joe Ball living on the premises and a room set apart for prisoners until they could be transferred to the Borough Gaol on Upper Mounts.

124. The Borough Gaol is seen in the background of this picture of Upper Mounts and the junction with Park Street. Seven murderers were executed at the Gaol, the last being a Peterborough tinsmith named John Eayrs who was hanged in 1914 for murdering his wife in a row about a halfpenny. The Gaol was demolished in the early 1930s. When this picture was taken the coloured population was small and this is one of the few pictures to include a black person.

NORTHAMPTON, FROM THE AIR.

"NORTHAMPTON INDEPENDENT" PHOTO.

125. An aerial view of the Gaol on Upper Mounts shows the main cell block and the circular exercise yard. The long building in the foreground was a factory with access from Earl Street, built in the 1880s. It overlooked the separate exercise yard for condemned prisoners awaiting execution and the owner used to charge a fee for any-one wishing to see the doomed prisoner at exercise.

The Chapel Court
Convent of Notre Dame
Northampton

126. When Notre Dame High School was demolished there was a wave of nostalgic regret but especially sad was the knocking down of the beautiful chapel in the grounds, without notice, in 1979. The only remaining vestige of the former use of the site, as a school and convent, is a small graveyard in which forty nuns were buried between 1852 and 1975. Now it stands by the pavement instead of in the placid surroundings of the gardens where its occupants used to stroll in peaceful contemplation. After the demolition it emerged that the chapel was not under a preservation order but the developer of the site was fined for knocking down some fine trees nearby.

127. This was the interior of the chapel of the Convent and School of Notre Dame in Abington Street.

128. St. Katharine's Church was built in 1839 as an overflow establishment to All Saints Church to cope with the growing population of the parish. The church was demolished in 1950 and the site is now grassed over as a Memorial Square to the dead of the Second World War, overlooked by the multi-storeyed Moat House Hotel and Barclaycard headquarters.

129. The interior of St. Katharine's Church. A small cairn of stones now marks where the altar stood.

130. Some of the most disorientating events for Northamptonians of the 20th century have concerned those elemental happenings of birth, marriage and death. For natives returning from abroad to see where they were born, where their parents were married and where they were buried, it has been disturbing to find that the streets they were born in have gone, that the church where their parents' wedding took place has disappeared, and that their 'last resting place' in the General Cemetery in Billing Road has been robbed of their tombstones. In the case of joint author Lou Warwick St. Edmund's Church (above) was the scene of the wedding of Thomas William Warwick and Lily Sproston on a Christmas Day during the First World War. Now it has gone completely.

131. Some of the 18th century advertisements in the Northampton Mercury indicate that the town had as much accommodation for horses as for people! There were some 4,000 inhabitants and the many inns had standing room for a similar number of horses. Horses remained fundamental to the transport scene until the 1920s and this picture is of a horse auction in the stables of the Peacock Hotel, on the east side of the Market Square. Conducting the sale is auctioneer Mr. Monty Marriott.

132. Although it was literally only a stone's throw from the Judge's Lodgings in George Row to All Saints Church where the Assize Services were held a coach and horses was provided for the Judge. It was supplied by the Frisby firm of the Peacock Stables and driven by Mr. Fred Harte. When the coach was withdrawn one judge refused the alternative motor car and walked. In the background are the premises of Boots the Chemists at the corner of Gold Street and the Drapery.

133. The last time that a four-in-hand team of horses pulled a hearse in Northampton was for the funeral of Mr. Robert Frisby on 7 April 1937. Driving the team was Mr. Frederick Harte who had been first horseman to Mr. Frisby at the Peacock Stables. He had also driven the town's horse-drawn fire engine. While Mr. Harte was away serving in the First World War a fire at Hardingstone Lodge had to be left to burn itself out because the engine could not be transported there. The RAC sign in this picture recalls the time when there was no one-way system round All Saints Church.

134. A line of funeral vehicles, probably taken in Cliftonville, belonging to the Frisby firm operating from the Peacock Stables, photographed by Henry Cooper. The earliest firm of undertakers in Northampton was that of W.G. Ward, founded about 1806 by Mr. J. Cooper, a cab proprietor. Another cab man, George Bonham, began providing a funeral service in the 1880s and this firm also carried Royal Mails until the Post Office acquired its own transport in about 1926.

135. Many Mayors and other leading citizens were laid to final rest in the General Cemetery in Billing Road, opened by a private company in 1847 with the Superintendent of Regents Park Botanical Gardens engaged to lay out a nine acre site providing for 16,575 graves. In 1959, with few spaces left, the company disclaimed the land which was taken over by Northampton Town Council who proceeded to smash up most of the memorials. It was another private company, with George Bernard Shaw as a principal shareholder, which set up the local crematorium, at Milton, in 1939.

136. Mark Dorman was among the Mayors of the town who were buried in the Billing Road Cemetery. During his Mayoralty Mr. Dorman opened the new Town Hall in 1864. He had come to Northampton from Ashford, Kent, and set up Dorman's Libraries in the Drapery. He married Charlotte, only daughter of Alderman Thomas Phipps, a member of the brewing family. He was unusual among Victorian Mayors in that one of his children, Frederick, was born during his Mayoralty – many Mayoral couples were too old for that to happen. Best known of his family was Thomas Phipps Dorman who owned the Opera House from 1889 to 1899. Mark Dorman died in 1877, aged 48.

137. A Mayor in a less formal setting is Alderman C.J. ('Charlie') Scott pictured on donkeyback in 1932 at a fete. His more normal form of locomotion was on a bicycle – he was an insurance representative. The first Labour Mayor of the town he also made history by broadcasting from the Town Hall to America, in connection with the 200th anniversary of the birth of George Washington, one of whose forbears, Lawrence Washington, was twice Mayor of Northampton in Elizabethan times.

138. Note the youth of some of the apprentices in this 1890s group of the staff of the Northampton Daily Chronicle and Northampton Herald. Proprietors Mr. James Butterfield and Mr. Henry Butterfield are in the centre. The weekly Herald had been set up in 1831 by Northamptonshire Tories opposed to the policies of the Northampton Mercury. In 1880 both camps had launched daily papers. In 1931 the four local publications were taken over by Provincial Newspapers Ltd. and merged into two – the daily Chronicle and Echo and weekly Mercury and Herald. Today both are part of United Newspapers Ltd. which recently acquired the Daily Express and Sunday Express.

139. Arriving in Northampton in 1931 with the difficult task of merging the town's two daily newspapers into the Chronicle and Echo and the two weeklies into the Mercury and Herald, was Mr. W. Cowper Barrons whose Scottish accent led to some problems of communications with his staff. He used to walk a mile or so into town from his homes, at first in Ardington Road and later in Billing Road. He also superintended the remarkable feat of continuous publication while the offices (as seen above) were rebuilt on the same site in 1939. The new buildings were swept away in 1978 when production moved to the present headquarters in Upper Mounts.

140. This picture is well outside the prescribed timespan of this collection, but is included to represent that latter-day period of holocaust when changes took place more fundamental than any of the 1880-1930 period, when whole districts were swept away along with all the associations and community spirit that went with them. It was called Expansion. The lower end of Newland (above) was where Lou Warwick walked daily to work for some thirty years. On the left at the corner with Princes Street was the former Temperance Hall Cinema, one of Britain's earliest, latterly used for bingo. Facing it was the 20th century Working Men's Club premises which the newspapers had planned to buy and expand into. It was a much narrower Newland up which Northamptonians escaped from the dreadful fire of 1675. Today the street has vanished beneath the Grosvenor Centre and the Greyfriars Bus Station.